Collins Primary Literacy

Pupil Book 3

Hazel Willard

Series editor: Kay Hiatt

Published by Collins
An imprint of HarperCollins*Publishers*
77–85 Fulham Palace Road
Hammersmith
London
W6 8JB

© HarperCollins*Publishers* Limited 2008

Series editor: Kay Hiatt

10 9 8 7 6 5 4 3 2 1

ISBN 978 0 00 722697 9

British Library Cataloguing in Publication Data
A Catalogue record for this publication is available from the British Library.

Acknowledgements
The authors and publishers wish to thank the following for permission to use copyright material:
Unit 1: A M Heath for text from *Whatever Happened at Winklesea?* by Helen Cresswell (Lutterworth Press); The Maggie Noach Literary Agency on behalf of the author for text from *A Family Like Mine* by Linda Newbery, edited by Kate Agnew (Egmont Books), text © Linda Newbery, 2003; Unit 2: Penguin Books for text from *Mr Majeika* by Humphrey Carpenter, text © Humphrey Carpenter, 1984 (Kestrel); Unit 3: Usborne Publishing Limited for text from *The Usborne Nature Trail Book of Birdwatching*, Copyright © Usborne Publishing Limited; The Royal Society for the Protection of Birds for text from *Migration Stories*, text © The Royal Society for the Protection of Birds, 2007; Unit 4: "Jigsaw Puddle" by Emily Hearn, text © Emily Hearn, reprinted with kind permission of the author; "Ice Cream and Fizzy Lemonade" by Stanley Cook from *Once I Ate a Jellyfish*, edited by John Foster (Blackie), text © The Estate of Stanley Cook; Unit 7: "Snake" by Keith Bosley, text © Keith Bosley, reprinted with kind permission of the author; Curtis Brown Limited for use of "Sky Day Dream" by Robert Froman from *Seeing Things: A Book of Poems* (HarperCollins), text © Robert Froman, 1974; Unit 8: Roald Dahl for text from *Danny The Champion of the World* by Roald Dahl (Jonathan Cape); Roald Dahl for text from *The Twits* by Roald Dahl (Puffin Books); AP Watt on behalf of Quentin Blake for illustrations from *Danny The Champion of the World* and *The Twits*; Unit 10: Usborne Publishing Limited for text from *Skull Island* by Lesley Sims, Copyright © Usborne Publishing Limited; Random House Group for text from *Jacqueline Hyde* by Robert Swindells (Doubleday); Unit 11: *Diwali* by Kerena Marchant (Wayland, 1996); HarperCollins for text and illustrations from *The Camel Fair* by Wendy Cooling, text © Wendy Cooling, 2005; Unit 12: "Riddle" by Judith Nicholls from *Storm's Eye* (OUP), text © Judith Nicholls, 1994, reprinted with kind permission of the author; "Teacher said" by Judith Nicholls from *Magic Mirror* (Faber and Faber), text © Judith Nicholls, 1985, reprinted with kind permission of the author

Illustrations: Sarah Horne, Beccy Blake, Tim Archbold, Shirley Chiang, Kevin Hopgood, Peter Bull

Photographs: p24, top right: Andy Holt; p80, left: Alamy/Louise Batalla Duran; p81, top right: Corbis/Reuters/Ajay Verma; p82, bottom: Corbis/Reuters/Kamal Kishore

Browse the complete Collins catalogue at
www.collinseducation.com

Printed in Hong Kong by Printing Express Ltd

Contents

1 Something Happened in My Street

In this unit, you'll find out how characters cope when faced with different situations and then you'll write about it.

Arriving at Winklesea

There is much excitement as the Kane family arrives at their holiday home – Dolphin caravan.

Then, almost before they knew it, they rounded a bend, and there lay the higgledy-piggledy roofs and chimneys of Winklesea below them, and beyond the wide shine of the sea.

"Oh, magic, magic," sang Mary. "We're coming, Winkie, we're coming!"

"A bit of hush now," said Mr Kane, "while I find the caravan."

"Straight to the sea front, Alfred," Mrs Kane told him, "and then left, to the dunes. That's what Fred said."

And so it was. They drew up in a small field beyond the town and could see the caravans tucked among the dunes, three or four of them. They all climbed out and stood in the salt, different air and felt a million miles away from home.

"You go and find ours, Dan and Mary," their mother said.

"Cream with a brown stripe, Fred said."

"Fred said Fred said Fred said!" sang Mary. They were off in a flash, in among the dunes, their feet slithering in the soft sand.

"And called Dolphin!" Mrs Kane's voice floated after them.

They didn't have to look far. They both spotted it together, cream with a brown stripe, and Dolphin painted in red by the door.

"Oh Dan!" whispered Mary. "Look – we shall see the sea!"

from **Whatever Happened at Winklesea?** *by* **Helen Cresswell**

1 Responding to the text

Answer the questions from the , or section.

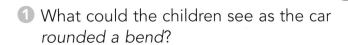

1. What could the children see as the car *rounded a bend*?

2. Why was Mary singing all the time?

3. Why do you think Mr Kane needed *a bit of hush*?

4. What feelings did they have as they got out of the car and smelled the sea air?

5. Describe Mary and Dan's caravan. What was it called?

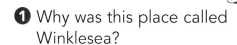

1. Why was this place called Winklesea?

2. Why was it a good idea to use the words *higgledy-piggledy* to describe the houses and chimneys?

3. Why did Mary call this place *Winkie*?

4. Why do you think everyone felt *a million miles away from home*?

5. Draw the whole family standing by their car, looking at the caravans and sniffing the sea air. Write a thought bubble for each character.

1. What words describe the roofs and chimneys of Winklesea?

2. Why do you think Mary sang *Oh magic, magic*?

3. What could Mary and Dan see as the car *rounded a bend*?

4. What do you think the children planned to do in Winklesea?

5. Think about the whole family standing by their car, looking at the caravans and sniffing the sea air. Talk to a friend about what they might say to each other.

2 Making a map

Read the description of Winklesea again. Draw your own map of Winklesea. Start with the bend in the road that leads into Winklesea, and end at the sea. Label your map with the words from the word bank below.

Useful words

Winklesea	sand dunes
road	sea
caravans	small field
Dolphin caravan	

3 Using adjectives to describe settings

Adjectives are words that describe nouns. The author uses the adjective *higgledy-piggledy* to describe the roofs in Winklesea.

Work in pairs. Think of some adjectives to describe each of the places on your map. Add them to the labels.

4 Writing a description of Winklesea

First draw two postcard shapes like the one below.

1 Fill in one shape with a picture of the sea at Winklesea. Remember to include the sand dunes and some caravans.

2 Imagine you are Mary or Dan writing a postcard to a friend. Write a few sentences in the other postcard shape to tell them about Winklesea and Dolphin caravan.

POSTCARD

Winklesea
27th July

Dear ...

Remember!

- Write in sentences. Start with a capital letter and end with a full stop.

- Use verbs, adjectives and description to make your sentences interesting.

- When you finish, check that your sentences make sense. Make any changes you need to.

Ivy Cottage

It's cold when twins Holly and Jonny and their parents arrive at Ivy Cottage in the middle of the countryside.

Ivy Cottage was miles down country lanes, then along a rutty track past a farm. The twins saw swelling hills and bare trees; they saw sheep, stiles and muddy paths. Dad stopped the car outside the farmhouse. The owner, Mrs Lamb, came out to give them the keys and show them the cottage. It stood in a ragged garden behind stone walls, with ivy scrambling over its porch. Inside was simple and old-fashioned but, Holly thought, rather cosy – or would be, when it was warmer. The floors had so many dips and rises that walking across them felt like being in a boat, and the stairs were narrow and twisty. The bedroom she was to share with Jonny had a window under the eaves, looking over the back garden.

Mrs Lamb, huddled in a fleece jacket, was explaining how to work the boiler.

"And you can have a log fire, if you like. There's plenty of logs outside, next to the stable – help yourself."

"A log fire – lovely!" Mum said, rubbing her hands. "Do you want to fetch some wood, twins, while I unpack?"

Holly's thoughts had fastened on the word *stable*. She thought for a wild moment there might be a pony in it, but the stable, at the end of an overgrown path, was empty. Still –

from A Family Like Mine by Linda Newbery

5 Exploring words

Work in pairs to find out what these words and phrases from *Ivy Cottage* mean.

rutty track	swelling hills	bare trees	stiles	ragged garden
ivy	scrambling	eaves	fleece	stable

Discuss what the word or phrase means with your partner. Write the word or phrase and write your definition next to it. Check in your dictionary. Revise your definition if you need to.

6 Using your senses

Imagine you are arriving at Ivy Cottage in winter. Use these headings to note down what you might see, hear, smell and feel.

What I see   What I hear   What I smell   What I feel

Now write your description of Ivy Cottage in full sentences.

Act out the scene in a group.

7 Think/pair/share

In pairs, discuss how Charlie and Ben feel about moving house. Copy the thought bubbles and label them *Charlie* and *Ben*. Write adjectives to show their feelings in each thought bubble. Think about the story *Charlie and Ben Move House*.

I feel ...

Charlie

I feel ...

Ben

Give some reasons for how they feel.

8 Spooky sentences

Play this game in pairs.

Build some spooky sentences. Take it in turns to read the sentences. When it's your turn, choose two adjectives from the box to add to each sentence. Make them as spooky as you dare!

scary	grey	old	tattered

crumbling	dusty	cobwebbed

murky	damp	freezing	grim

The spooky house was dark and silent. The door swung open. I walked through its rooms one by one.

The first room was _____ and _____.

The second room was _____ and _____.

The third room was _____ and _____.

Then I ran out of the back door and raced home as fast as I could!

Write more spooky sentences for the fourth, fifth and sixth rooms.

9 Writing a story with a familiar setting

Have you ever moved home? If you have, write a short story in three paragraphs about:

❶ your feelings as you leave your old home.

❷ a description of your new home.

❸ your feelings about your new home.

If you have never moved home, imagine you are Charlie and write a short story in three paragraphs about:

❶ Charlie's feelings as he leaves his old home.

❷ a description of his home.

❸ his feelings about his new home.

Remember!

- Write in full sentences.
- Start each sentence with a capital letter and end with a full stop.
- Each sentence should have a verb and it should make sense.
- Give reasons for your feelings.

What I have learned

- I understand what a familiar setting is.
- I can draw and describe a familiar setting.
- I can explain why settings affect how characters feel.
- I can write or tell a short story in a familiar setting.

2

Speaking Loud and Clear

In this unit, you'll learn about how speech is written in stories and plays and then write a scene for a play.

Hamish Bigmore and the Frog

Mr Majeika is a teacher who is also a secret magician.

On the Wednesday morning before Hamish Bigmore's mother and father were due to come home, Mr Majeika was giving Class Three a nature-study lesson, with the tadpoles in the glass tank that sat by his desk. Hamish Bigmore was being ruder than ever.

"Does anyone know how long tadpoles take to turn into frogs?" Mr Majeika asked Class Three.

"Haven't the slightest idea," said Hamish Bigmore.

"Please," said Melanie, holding up her hand, "I don't think it's very long. Only a few weeks."

"*You* should know," sneered Hamish Bigmore. "You look just like a tadpole yourself."

Melanie began to cry.

"Be quiet, Hamish Bigmore," said Mr Majeika. "Melanie is quite right. It all happens very quickly. The tadpoles grow arms and legs, and very soon –"

"I shouldn't think they'll grow at all if they see *you* staring in at them through the glass," said Hamish Bigmore to Mr Majeika. "Your face would frighten them to death!"

"Hamish Bigmore, I have had enough of you," said Mr Majeika. "Will you stop behaving like this?"

"No, I won't!" said Hamish Bigmore.

Mr Majeika pointed a finger at him.

And Hamish Bigmore vanished.

There was complete silence. Class Three stared at the empty space where Hamish Bigmore had been sitting.

Then Pandora Green pointed at the glass tank, and began to shout: "Look! Look! A frog! A frog! One of the tadpoles has turned into a frog!"

Mr Majeika looked closely at the tank. Then he put his head in his hands. He seemed very upset.

"No, Pandora," he said. "It isn't one of the tadpoles. It's Hamish Bigmore."

For a moment, Class Three were struck dumb. Then everyone burst out laughing. "Hooray! Hooray! Hamish Bigmore has been turned into a frog! Good old Mr Magic!"

"It looks like Hamish Bigmore, doesn't it?" Pete said to Thomas. Certainly the frog's expression looked very much like Hamish's face. And it was splashing noisily around the tank and carrying on in the silly sort of way that Hamish did.

Mr Majeika looked very worried. "Oh dear, oh dear," he kept saying.

"Didn't you mean to do it?" said Jody.

Mr Majeika shook his head. "Certainly not. I quite forgot myself. It was a complete mistake."

"Well," said Thomas, "you can turn him back again, can't you?"

Mr Majeika shook his head again. "I'm not at all sure that I can," he said.

Thomas and Pete looked at him in astonishment.

"You see," he went on, "it was an old spell, something I learnt years and years ago and thought I'd forgotten. I don't know what were the exact words I used. And, as I am sure you understand, it's not possible to undo a spell unless you know exactly what the words were."

"So Hamish Bigmore may have to stay a frog?" said Pete. "That's the best thing I've heard for ages!"

Mr Majeika shook his head. "For you, maybe, but not for him. I'll have to try and do *something*." And he began to mutter a whole series of strange-sounding words under his breath.

All kinds of things began to happen. The room went dark, and the floor seemed to rock. Green smoke came out of an empty jar on Mr Majeika's desk. He tried some more words, and this time there was a small thunderstorm in the sky outside. But nothing happened to the frog.

"Oh dear," sighed Mr Majeika, "what *am* I going to do?"

from **Mr Majeika** *by Humphrey Carpenter*

 ## 1 Responding to the text

Answer the questions from the , or section.

1. What did Mr Majeika ask the children about tadpoles?

2. Why did Melanie cry?

3. What did the children shout when Hamish Bigmore had been turned into a frog?

4. How do you know when someone is speaking in a story?

5. Why do you think Mr Majeika *put his head in his hands*?

6. Think of words to use instead of *said* in this sentence:

    "Didn't you mean to do it?" said Jody.

1 What did Hamish Bigmore say to upset Melanie?

2 How do you know that Mr Majeika was cross?

3 Why do you think Mr Majeika was worried when Hamish Bigmore vanished?

4 Make up some words you would use for a spell to change the frog back into Hamish.

5 Why do you think Pete said the frog looked like Hamish Bigmore?

6 What happened when Mr Majeika muttered strange sounding words?

1 What did Hamish Bigmore say to really hurt the feelings of Mr Majeika?

2 How do you think Hamish might behave towards his parents?

3 Write down what Mr Majeika might have been thinking as he held his head in his hands.

4 Have you ever been *struck dumb*? What was happening at the time?

5 How can someone forget themselves, like Mr Majeika said?

6 Give one reason why Hamish should remain as a frog and one reason why he should be changed back again.

2 Role play

Work in pairs. One of you is going to role play as Jody and the other will be Jody's friend from another class. Remember the rules of conversation.

Jody	Jody's friend
Tell your friend what happened in class when Hamish Bigmore turned into a frog.	Ask Jody questions about what happened and listen to her answers.

3 Who is speaking?

In stories, spoken words are put inside speech marks.

For example:

"No, I won't!" said Hamish Bigmore.

In cartoons, spoken words are put inside speech bubbles, without speech marks.

Follow the instructions from the , or ▲ section.

Read what Mr Majeika is saying and write it in a sentence with speech marks.

Read what Mr Majeika and Pandora Green are saying and write it in sentences with speech marks. What else do you think Mr Majeika might say? Write it in a sentence with speech marks.

Read what each of the characters are saying and write it in sentences with speech marks.

Write what each of the characters might say next, in sentences with speech marks.

4 Finding speech verbs

All the words in the bubble are verbs. Find the verbs that show someone is speaking. (Clue: there are ten speech verbs.)

grumbled	smiled	murmured
shook	asked	groaned
croaked	did	moaned
yelled	went	shouted
looked	cried	shook
whispered	jumped	started

❶ Find the ten speech verbs and write them in a list.

❷ Choose the best speech verb from your list to complete this sentence.

"Don't make a sound," _____ Jody.

❸ Choose the best speech verbs to complete these sentences.

"I feel very odd," _____ Hamish Bigmore.

"Oh dear," _____ Mr Majeika. "I've done something terrible."

❹ Choose four speech verbs and use them in your own sentences.

5 Turning a story into a play

You are going to turn part of *Hamish Bigmore and the Frog* into a playscript. Work in pairs. First, plan your playscript.

- Check what characters will be in the play and list their names.

- Next, check where the play is set.

- Decide what scene this is – Scene 1, Scene 2 or Scene 3.

- Write a number and title for the scene (for example: *Scene 2: The Problem*).

- Write a title for the setting (for example: *The Classroom*).

- Write who is speaking first and then what they are saying.

Turn over to find the story you are going to turn into a playscript.

Turn this part of the story into a playscript. Follow the tips from the previous page. Rehearse your ideas with your partner before writing them down.

Mr Majeika was giving Class Three a nature study lesson.

"Does anyone know how long tadpoles take to turn into frogs?" Mr Majeika asked.

"Haven't the slightest idea," said Hamish Bigmore.

"Please," said Melanie holding up her hand. "I don't think it's very long. Only a few weeks."

"*You* should know," sneered Hamish Bigmore. "You look just like a tadpole yourself."

"Hamish Bigmore, I have had enough of you," said Mr Majeika. "Will you stop behaving like this?"

"No, I won't!" said Hamish.

Mr Majeika pointed a finger at him and Hamish Bigmore vanished.

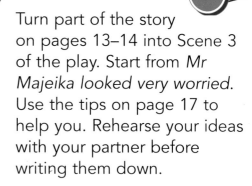

Turn part of the story on pages 13–14 into Scene 3 of the play. Start from *Mr Majeika looked very worried.* Use the tips on page 17 to help you. Rehearse your ideas with your partner before writing them down.

Remember!

- You don't need to use speech marks.
- Use exclamation marks to show surprise, or question marks if you want the character to ask a question.
- The dialogue should tell the story.
- Try reading your scene aloud to check it makes sense.

What I have learned

- I understand the differences between stories and plays.
- I can identify and use speech verbs.
- I can write dialogue.
- I can change part of a story into a playscript.

Garden Birds

In this unit, you'll find out about presenting information about birds and write a non-chronological report.

Nesting birds

Find out where birds make their nests and how you can tell if a bird is nesting.

The nesting season is a time of great activity for all birds. First they have to find a place where they can build their nests and feed. This area then becomes their territory. When they have found a mate, they have to build a nest, lay eggs and rear their young. With all this going on, it is not difficult to find out when and where a bird is building its nest or feeding its young. A bird carrying something in its beak is the most common sign.

The song thrush builds its nest in a bush. There are usually four or five eggs. Both parents feed the young birds with worms and snails. The adult bird arrives at the nest with food. It pushes the food into the mouth of one of the young birds, removes any droppings from the nest and flies off to collect more food.

When a parent bird approaches the nest, the young birds beg for food with wide, open mouths.

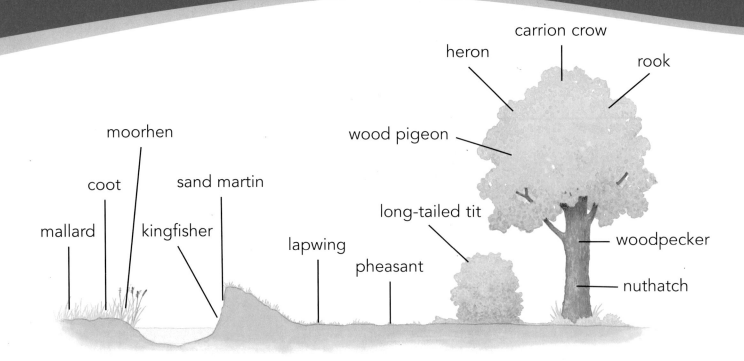

In the country, birds nest in many different places. They use trees and hedges, the shelter of steep banks and holes in trees. Some birds, like the lapwing, make hardly any nest at all. They lay their eggs in a shallow hole in the ground.

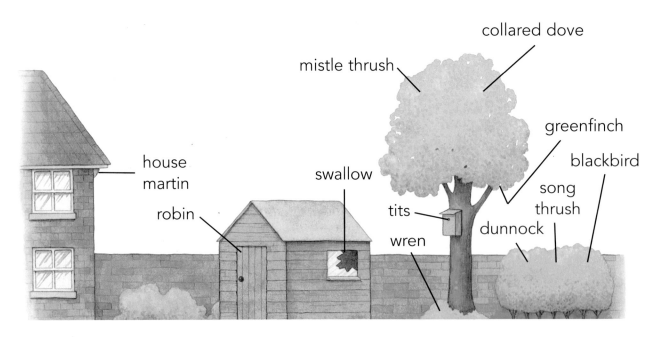

Many birds nest in gardens but only in sheltered places, safe from cats and dogs. They use thick bushes, trees, ivy-covered walls and sheds as well as nesting boxes. Some birds, like the house martin, even build under the roof.

from **The Usborne Nature Trail Book of Birdwatching**

1 Responding to the text

Answer the questions from the , or  section.

1. Why is the nesting season a busy time for birds?

2. What is the most common sign that birds are nesting?

3. Look at the diagram showing nests in the garden and find out where house martins nest.

4. Where do sand martins nest?

5. Which fact did you find most interesting?

1. Write a list of what birds have to do in the nesting season.

2. Why do you think some birds nest in high trees?

3. What dangers could face lapwings, pheasants and wrens?

4. Why do many birds nest in bushes?

5. Which fact did you find most interesting?

1. Look at the diagrams in the text and find out where these birds nest: woodpeckers, rooks, lapwings, sand martins and moorhens.

2. Write a list of what birds have to do in the nesting season:

    1. Find a place...

    2.

    3

    4.

    5.

3. What do song thrushes feed to their young?

4. Which fact did you find most interesting?

2 Using diagrams to make notes

Make your own chart showing the places that birds nest and different types of birds. Use the information in the diagrams on page 20 to fill in this chart.

Birds' nesting places

NESTING PLACE / BIRD	Trees	Hedges	Ground	Holes in banks	Sheds and houses
Blackbird					
Carrion crow					
Wood pigeon					
Moorhen					
Long-tailed tit					
Greenfinch					
Heron					
House martin					
Kingfisher					

Choose two more birds from the diagrams to add to the list.

Choose five more birds from the diagrams to add to the list.

3 Finding information in diagrams

Draw a large hedge. Label birds that nest in hedges on your diagram. Use your chart and the words in the word box to help you.

Draw a large tree and label the birds that nest in trees on your diagram. Use the information in your chart to help you.

Word box

long-tailed tit   blackbird

dunnock   song thrush

4 Role play

In a group of four, choose one pair to be experts on nesting birds and the other pair to ask questions. Take turns to ask each other questions about the birds you have listed on your charts.

Migration stories

Some birds make the most incredible journeys every year.

Cuckoo

Cuckoos are summer visitors to the UK from tropical Africa. They arrive between mid-April and early May, when you can hear their well-known cuckoo call in most parts of the countryside though the birds themselves can be hard to spot.

Cuckoos have a crafty breeding strategy. Instead of building their own nest, they use the nests of host birds, such as dunnocks and meadow pipits. When a female cuckoo finds a suitable nest, and the hosts aren't looking, she removes one of their eggs and lays her own egg in its place.

Young cuckoos must find their own way to Africa.

The young cuckoo hatches after only 12 days and quickly pushes the hosts' eggs or babies out of the nest. After 19 days it leaves the nest, but the hosts continue to feed it for two more weeks, by which time it has grown much bigger than them.

Adult cuckoos are among the earliest of our summer visitors to leave. They have no need to help rear their young, so they are free to go. Most leave the UK during July. Young cuckoos leave about one month later, when they are fully fledged. They never see their parents.

We don't know much about cuckoo migration routes. Cuckoos from the UK probably travel down through central Europe to the south of Italy, where they feed up before crossing to Africa. Some scientists think that they then cross the Mediterranean and Sahara in a single flight of over 3,000 km (1,875 miles).

The only ringed cuckoo recaptured in Africa was from Cameroon, in central Africa, but we know that many travel farther south than this. In Africa, cuckoos never call, so most probably go unnoticed.

from Migration Stories *by The Royal Society for the Protection of Birds*

5 Exploring unfamiliar words

Work in pairs. Read these sentences carefully and talk to your partner about the meaning of the words in **bold**. If you get stuck, use your dictionary.

Sometimes information texts contain unfamiliar words. Reading around the word can help you understand the meaning.

Answer all the questions. Write a sentence of your own to explain the meaning of each word in **bold**.

Answer questions **2** and **3**.

Write a sentence of your own to explain the meaning of the word *migration*.

❶ Cuckoos have a crafty breeding strategy. Instead of building their own nest, they use other birds' nests for laying their eggs.
Do you think **breeding** means:

a) building a nest?

b) going to sleep?

c) having young chicks?

crafty = sly

strategy = plan

❷ Cuckoos use a nest belonging to **host** birds, such as dunnocks and meadow pipits.
Do you think **host** means:

a) the bird who has made its own nest and looks after the cuckoo's eggs?

b) a good nest builder?

❸ We don't know much about cuckoo **migration** routes. They probably fly down through central Europe to the south of Italy.
Do you think **migration** means:

a) feeding?

b) flying to another country?

c) singing?

routes = flight paths

6 Using the present tense in an information text

Non-chronological reports describe something that keeps happening, so they are written in the present tense.

Read these sentences. Then follow the instructions for

 , or .

1 The nesting season **was** a time of great activity for all song thrushes.

2 Blue whales **will be** the biggest creatures on earth.

3 Kangaroos **lived** in Australia.

4 House martins **will make** nests in houses.

5 Song thrush parents **will feed** their young birds with worms and snails.

6 Lapwings **laid** their eggs in a shallow hole in the ground.

Change the tense of the verb to the present tense in sentence 1 and sentence 3.

Change the tense to the present tense in all six sentences. Underline the verb and talk to your partner about how it has changed.

Choose four sentences and change the tense to the present tense. Talk to your partner about how the verb has changed.

7 Using a writing frame

You're going to write your own report about a bird. Follow the instructions for 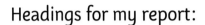 , ⬤ or ▲ .

Headings for my report:

Title

Introduction

Description

Habitat

Lifestyle

Interesting information

Labelled diagram

Work in pairs. Choose a bird. Find the information for each heading. Discuss what you want to write with your partner before starting. Write one sentence for each heading.

Choose a bird. Practise writing a sentence on your mini-whiteboard before finding information for each heading. Write one sentence for each heading. Draw a diagram and add labels to show information.

Choose a bird. Use the headings to help you with your writing. Write two sentences for each heading. Draw a diagram and add labels to show information.

Remember!

- Use the present tense.
- Write in sentences.
- Each heading should describe something different.
- Use labelled diagrams to show information in a different way.

What I have learned

- I can make notes on a non-fiction text and write down the key words.
- I can label a diagram.
- I can take part in role play.
- I can write my own non-fiction report about a garden bird.

Sights, Sounds and Feelings

In this unit, you'll read poems about senses and feelings, and write a poem about your own feelings.

Jigsaw Puddle

Sloshing my boat in the pavement puddle
I jiggle the sky above,
I fold the clouds in a sheep-like huddle,
I bobble the sun in the blue and white muddle —
And then I stand still —
Till the jigsaw puddle
Is smooth as a mirror again.

Emily Hearn

Ice Cream and Fizzy Lemonade

Ice cream is sliding, soft and cold
And gives a smooth and soothing coat
On hot summer days
To the back of your throat.

Fizzy lemonade looks like water
But as you unscrew the bottle top
Bubbles crowd together in froth
With a rushing sound and a sudden pop.

It prickles and tickles your nose
And tingles the back of your throat
That needs another sliding soft ice cream
To give it back a smooth and soothing coat.

Stanley Cook

1 Responding to the text

Answer the questions from the , or section.

① Say the word *sloshing* three times. What does it make you think of?

② Why does the child like *sloshing my boat in the pavement puddle*?

③ Read the poem by Stanley Cook. What does ice cream feel like when you swallow it?

④ What does fizzy lemonade feel like in your mouth?

---

① In *Jigsaw Puddle*, why did the poet describe the clouds as looking like sheep?

② Which words does Stanley Cook use to describe the way ice cream feels in your mouth?

③ Say these words quietly three times: *smooth* and *soothing*. Why did the poet choose these words?

④ Find the words that exactly describe what happens to the bubbles as the bottle top is unscrewed. Draw a picture of what happens.

---

① Why do you think the poem is called *Jigsaw Puddle*?

② Why did the poet choose these verbs: *jiggle*, *fold* and *bobble*.

③ Read the poem by Stanley Cook. Which words describe how ice cream feels in your mouth?

④ Say why the poet chose these verbs about lemonade: *prickles* and *tickles* and *tingles*.

⑤ What noises are made by lemonade?

Sounds

The whistling of the wind,
The pattering of the rain,
The tapping of the hail-stones
Upon the window-pane.

The splashing of your gum-boots
In the puddles of the lane.
The gurgling of the water
As it rushes down the drain.

The cooing of the pigeon,
The crying of the eagle,
The snorting and the sniffing
And the barking of the beagle.

The slam of a large door,
The slam of a small,
The crack of a rifle,
The bounce of a ball.

The very very quiet sounds –
The walking of some ants;
The very very noisy sounds –
The run of elephants.

Alexander Kennedy

2 Finding loud and quiet verbs

Read aloud the poem *Sounds* and use your voice to show the loud and quiet sounds. Look for the loud and quiet verbs.

Make a list of all the loud and quiet verbs that you can find in the poem. Then think of some more loud and quiet verbs of your own.

Loud verbs	Quiet verbs
barking	cooing
splashing	pattering

3 Finding out about synonyms

A synonym is a word or phrase that means exactly or nearly the same as another.

Some of the words in the box below are synonyms. Work with your partner to sort the words into three groups of synonyms. Say why you've put each group of words together.

sip   gulp   taste   devour
chew   slurp   bake
boil   guzzle   suck   swallow
cook   braise   grill
fry

Now think of ten synonyms for the verb *talk*.

Night Time Nasties

Sometimes at night
When sleep won't come,
I hear strange noises that make my flesh numb.

The tick, tock, tick of the clock in the hall
Is the rhythm of feet as they stealthily fall,
Creeping, closer towards my bed.

But I know it's only in my head.

Long shadows of leaves on the window pane
Is a demon creature climbing the drain,
Clawing, closer towards my bed.

But I know it's only in my head.

The swish of the tyres on the busy M3
Is the cloak of a shadow man swirling round me,
Creeping closer towards my bed.

But I know it's only in my head.

The whistles and grunts of dad as he snores
Is a raging beast with raucous roars,
Charging closer towards my bed.

But I know it's only in my head.

I know it's only in my head
But the nasties are nudging towards my bed.
They thrive in the dark, the velvety black.

But they'll disappear at daylight's crack
When the first blackbird chatters.
They'll shiver and sigh,
Fading away, as they wither and die.

But they're waiting to pounce,
They're ready to bite.

Quickly, quickly, turn on the light!

Hazel Willard

4 Independent writing

You are going to write your own verse for the poem *Night Time Nasties*. Copy the table.

Night Time Nasties	Picture	Caption
What is really happening?		The clock is ticking in the hall.
What does the poet imagine is happening?		Someone is creeping along the hall.
What is really happening?		
What does the poet imagine is happening?		

❶ Add some everyday noises of your own to the table and draw pictures of them. Imagine what the noises *might* sound like at night and draw a picture. Write captions for your pictures.

❷ Write your verse for *Night Time Nasties*. Use the table to help you. Start each line like this:

Line 1: I can hear …
Line 2: It sounds like …
Line 3: But I know it's only in my head!

Remember!

Use words to create interesting effects:

• loud and quiet verbs

• rhyme and repetition

• adjectives and synonyms

• alliteration.

Read your verse aloud to see how it sounds.

What I have learned

• I can recognise and use verbs and synonyms.

• I can read and understand how some poems use interesting words.

• I can write a poem about my feelings using interesting words.

Fantastic Creatures!

In this unit, you'll learn about fables and myths from around the world and write your own sequel to a Greek myth.

Odysseus and Polyphemus

Odysseus is a famous hero in the myths of Ancient Greece. A myth is a story which isn't based on historical fact and often features gods, goddesses and fantastic creatures. This story tells what happens when Odysseus and his crew take shelter in the cave of the giant Cyclops, Polyphemus.

Polyphemus was a Cyclops, and the son of the god of the sea, Poseidon. The Cyclops were giants who had only one eye in the centre of their foreheads. They lived alone in caves on the far away island of Sicily, looking after goats and sheep.

Odysseus and his crew were on their way home after fighting in the Trojan War and decided to land on an island to stock up with food and water for the journey. They found

Polyphemus's cave and went inside hoping to steal some food. Odysseus had always wanted to see a Cyclops, so he and his crew hid in the cave until Polyphemus returned.

Later that evening, Polyphemus the giant returned to his cave with his flock of sheep and rolled a huge boulder in front of the entrance. When Odysseus and his men saw the giant, they gasped in amazement and the giant heard them. Enraged to see strangers in his cave, he scooped the nearest men up in his huge hands and devoured them for his dinner. After that, he fell fast asleep.

When the giant awoke the next morning, he ate more of the crew for his breakfast, rolled back the boulder, counted his flock of sheep out of the cave one by one, and took them off to graze. Of course, he didn't forget to roll the boulder back before he left, trapping the men inside.

Odysseus and his men were not strong enough to move the boulder in order to escape. He needed to think of another way to save them.

That night, Odysseus waited until Polyphemus was asleep. Then he and four of his men plunged a red-hot pole into Polyphemus's eye and blinded him.

At dawn, Odysseus and what was left of his crew crawled underneath each of the giant's sheep and clung fast to their bellies. The blind Polyphemus rolled the boulder away from the cave and counted his sheep as they trotted out of the cave by patting their backs. One by one the sheep left the cave, carrying the men safely beneath them. Odysseus and his men had escaped!

However, Odysseus did not know that Polyphemus was the son of Poseidon. The sea god was furious with Odysseus and sent many terrible storms to make sure that Odysseus spent the next ten years wandering the world, unable to get home to the beautiful island of Ithica.

Hazel Willard

1 Responding to the text

Answer the questions from the , or section.

1. What is a myth?

2. Draw a picture of Polyphemus.

3. How did Polyphemus stop Odysseus and his crew from leaving the cave?

4. What did Odysseus do to Polyphemus?

5. Do you think Odysseus had a clever plan? Why?

1. Who was Polyphemus's father?

2. Was Polyphemus pleased to see Odysseus and his crew? Why not?

3. Why do you think Odysseus and his crew stayed in Polyphemus's cave?

4. How did Odysseus trick Polyphemus?

5. How did Odysseus suffer for his clever plan to trick Polyphemus?

6. Do you like Odysseus? Why/why not?

1. Write a few sentences explaining who the Cyclops were.

2. Why do you think Polyphemus was enraged when he saw strangers in his cave?

3. What was Odysseus's plan?

4. Why do you think Odysseus blinded Polyphemus?

5. Was Odysseus right to blind the giant?

6. What else could Odysseus have done to outwit the giant?

2 Story hands

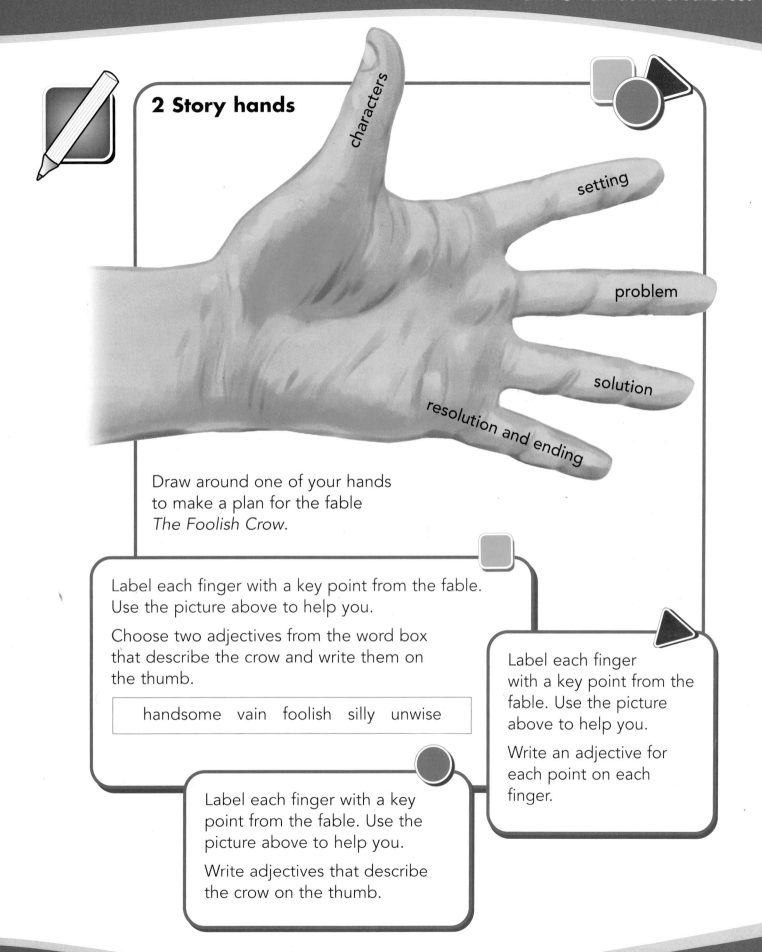

characters

setting

problem

solution

resolution and ending

Draw around one of your hands to make a plan for the fable *The Foolish Crow*.

Label each finger with a key point from the fable. Use the picture above to help you.

Choose two adjectives from the word box that describe the crow and write them on the thumb.

handsome	vain	foolish	silly	unwise

Label each finger with a key point from the fable. Use the picture above to help you.

Write an adjective for each point on each finger.

Label each finger with a key point from the fable. Use the picture above to help you.

Write adjectives that describe the crow on the thumb.

3 WANTED!

Polyphemus is wanted by the police. Design a WANTED! poster for him. Draw a picture of Polyphemus and label it with adjectives that describe him.

You can use adjectives from the box or choose your own.

gigantic
one-eyed
fierce
huge
angry
hungry
violent
cunning

Add some captions and sentences to describe Polyphemus.

For example: *Wanted! The one-eyed giant Polyphemus, who is very violent and likes to eat humans.*

4 Poseidon

Read this description of Poseidon, who was Polyphemus's father. Poseidon was also known as Neptune.

Poseidon was the god of the sea. He lived in a palace made of coral on the ocean floor. He drove a chariot (a two-wheeled cart) pulled by horses. He was very moody and, when he was in a bad temper, he hit the sea with his trident (a three-pronged fork) and caused earthquakes, storms and shipwrecks. People said he made sailors drown at sea. He hated Odysseus because he had blinded Polyphemus and tried to stop him from returning home to Ithica.

Draw a picture of Poseidon. Label it with words that you think would describe him.

Draw a picture of Poseidon and label it with words that you think would describe him. Then write two sentences describing Poseidon.

5 Odysseus and Polyphemus meet again!

Imagine that Odysseus and Polyphemus meet again. What do you think they might say to each other?

Draw your own picture of Odysseus and Polyphemus.

Draw speech bubbles coming out of their mouths.

Write what you think they would say in the speech bubbles.

Make a comic strip to show the conversation that Odysseus and Polyphemus might have had.

Draw your own pictures of Odysseus and Polyphemus.

Draw speech bubbles coming out of their mouths.

Write what you think they would say in the speech bubbles.

6 Writing a sequel to the myth

Use your story plan to help you write a sequel to *Odysseus and Polyphemus*, to tell the story of Polyphemus's revenge.

characters

1. **Characters:** Odysseus, sailors, Polyphemus

setting

2. **Setting:** Polyphemus's island

problem

3. **Problem:** Odysseus is blown back to Polyphemus's island and the giant wants revenge.

solution

4. **Solution:** Odysseus has another plan to outwit the giant.

resolution and ending

5. **Ending:** A Greek god helps Odysseus. He and his crew escape.

Remember!

- Think of a good opening for your story.
- Use powerful verbs and interesting adjectives.
- Try to bring the reader into the story by using a phrase like "What could he do?"
- Indent the line to show you are writing a new paragraph.

Give your sequel a new title and start a new paragraph for each of the five key points.

You can use the paragraph beginnings on the next page to help you, or choose your own.

Paragraph 1: Describe the characters who are going to be in the story

Odysseus had tricked Polyphemus. The giant's father, Poseidon, was furious …

Paragraph 2: This is where the story will be taking place

Polyphemus was on his island …

Paragraph 3: The problem the characters face in the story

Polyphemus saw Odysseus's boat, a wreck on the shore …

Paragraph 4: How the characters sort out the problem

A goddess saw Odysseus and felt so sorry for him that she …

Paragraph 5: Give your story a good ending

Once again, Odysseus and his crew were able to leave the island.

What I have learned

- I understand what fables and myths are.
- I can talk about the words used and sequence the stories.
- I can write a sequel to a Greek myth.

6

This Is What You Do

In this unit, you'll read, follow and write instructions.

Games

Achi

Achi is a game played by children in Ghana.

Number of players: two

Equipment: a board as shown

four counters each (a different colour for each player)

Rules:

1. The aim of this game is to get three counters in a line. The players take turns to place one of their counters on a point where lines join.

2. When all eight counters have been placed, each player may move along a line to an empty point.

3. The winner is the first player to get three counters in a row, down, across or diagonally.

Nine Men's Morris

This is a very old game for two players.

Equipment: a board as shown

nine counters each

Rules:

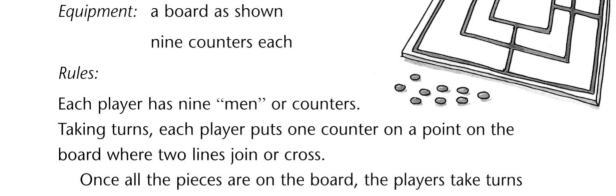

Each player has nine "men" or counters.
Taking turns, each player puts one counter on a point on the
board where two lines join or cross.

Once all the pieces are on the board, the players take turns
in moving a man from one point to an empty point which is next
door to it and joined directly by a line. Each time a player gets three
men in a row, he or she may remove one of the other player's men.

One player wins when the other has just two men left, or when
the other is blocked and unable to move.

1 Responding to the text

Answer the questions from the , or section.

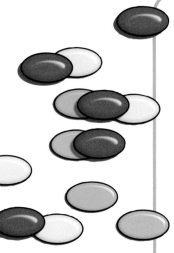

1. Which country does the game *Achi* come from?

2. How many people can play *Achi*?

3. Who is the winner in *Achi*?

4. Which game do you think is the most fun to play? Why?

5. Tell your friend about your favourite game and why you like it.

---

1. How are the rules for the two games similar?

2. How are the rules for the two games different?

3. Which game do you think would be most fun to play?

4. Who is the winner in *Nine Men's Morris*?

5. Does *Achi* remind you of another well-known game? What is it?

---

1. How is *Nine Men's Morris* different from *Achi* in the way it is written?

2. Which instructions do you prefer? Why?

3. Make a list of all the verbs in *Nine Men's Morris*.

4. If you had to rewrite *Nine Men's Morris* as a set of numbered instructions, how many instructions do you think you would need?

5. What do you think would be the first instruction for *Nine Men's Morris*? Write it out.

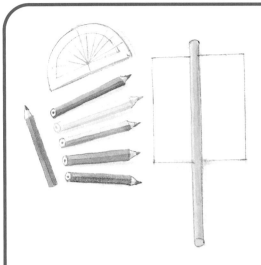

Vanishing colours

White light is made up of all the colours of the rainbow. This disc will make those colours change back into white or a pale grey.

You will need: card, protractor, crayons, a piece of wooden rod about 15 cm long.

❶ Cut out a disc from the card.

❷ Divide it into six equal parts, using a protractor. Each segment should have an angle of 60 degrees.

❸ Colour the segments in the order these colours appear in the rainbow: red, orange, yellow, green, blue and violet.

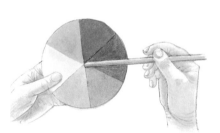

❹ Make a hole in the centre of the disc and carefully push the wooden rod through so that it is fairly tight.

❺ Hold the rod between your hands with the colours facing up. Rub your hands back and forth to spin the disc, and watch what happens.

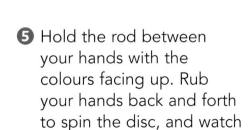

2 Making a flow chart

In pairs, discuss and plan how to give instructions for a simple classroom task. The example here is for watering a plant. Choose one of your own. Together, make a flow chart from your instructions for this task.

1. Find a watering can or other container suitable for holding water.

2. Fill the container with water.

3. Carefully pour the water into the plant pot. Don't give it too much at one time.

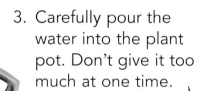

4. Check the soil with your fingertips to see if it needs more water.

3 Bossy verbs!

Instructions tell people **exactly** what to do.

The verbs are bossy, for example: *Cut, Divide, Colour, Make, Hold.*

Find these bossy verbs in the *Vanishing colours* instructions on page 45.

Chocolate coconut balls

First of all you need to mix the coconut and sugar with milk.

The instruction above is too long – there are no bossy verbs.
It should be written like this:

Mix the coconut and sugar with the milk.

Choose the correct bossy verb from the list and copy out the recipe.

| Lift   Melt   Place   Make   Coat |

1. Mix the coconut and sugar with the milk.
2. _____ small balls from the mixture.
3. _____ chocolate in a small wooden basin.
4. _____ balls in the chocolate.
5. _____ out the balls one by one with a fork.
6. _____ the balls on waxed paper.

Write your own set of instructions for making your favourite sandwich.

Write down your choice of ingredients, followed by your set of instructions.

Underline all your bossy verbs in red.

My Favourite Sandwich
You will need:

4 Writing instructions

Write your own instructions for doing one of these things.

How to make a cup of tea

How to use a phone

How to make a sandwich

How to send an email

How to record a TV programme

Remember!

- Number each stage.
- When you've finished, check that you haven't missed anything out, and that everything is in the right order.

For example:

1. Put water in the kettle and switch it on.
2. Put a teabag in the teapot.
3. …

5 Writing a recipe

1 Write a recipe for one of your favourite dishes. Use these headings to help you:

> Ingredients
>
> Equipment
>
> Steps

2 Make up a magic recipe with horrible ingredients. Use headings for your recipe.

Remember!

- Think carefully *before* you write.

- Imagine you are telling someone else what to do.

- Check your plan – does it make sense?

- Are your instructions in the correct order?

6 Giving the rules of the game

Games need to have very clear rules for all players. You're going to write the rules of a game for a younger child to follow. Work in pairs and use the headings to help you.

Name of the game:

Number of players:

Equipment:

Aim of the game:

How the game starts:

How to play:

1.

2.

3.

4.

How the game finishes:

Remember!

- Keep your instructions simple.
- Try reading them aloud to check they make sense.
- Think about who you're writing the rules for (a younger child).
- Choose a game you know really well, like Noughts and Crosses.
- Make your rules as clear and simple as possible.
- Don't forget to write about the aim of the game.
- Draw pictures or diagrams if you think they'll make the rules clearer.

What I have learned

- I understand how instruction texts are organised.
- I can use the language of instruction texts, especially bossy verbs.
- I can set out instruction texts and write my own sequenced instructions for others to follow.

7

All Shapes and Sizes

In this unit, you'll read, perform and write shape poems and calligrams.

1 Making calligrams

Calligrams are words that have been written in a way that shows what they mean. Here some examples:

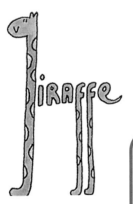

Write each of these words in a shape to show its meaning:

| fat | wobble | tail | stretch |

Make a picture from each of these words to show its meaning:

| cold | shivering | bang | crash |

This is an example of a calligram of an antonym (opposite):

Ancient
Modern

Make calligrams of these antonyms:

big – small

thick – thin

wide – narrow

steady – shaky

Shape poems

Shape poems are written in the shape of what the poem is about.

Snake

Snake glides
   through grass
      over
         pebbles
           forked tongue
      working
     never
  speaking
    but its
      body
        whispers
          listen.

Keith Bosley

Sky Day Dream

WITH THEM
COULD FLY OFF
I WISHED THAT I
INTO THE SKY
FLY OFF
SOME CROWS
ONCE I SAW

Robert Froman

Mosquito

Mozzie

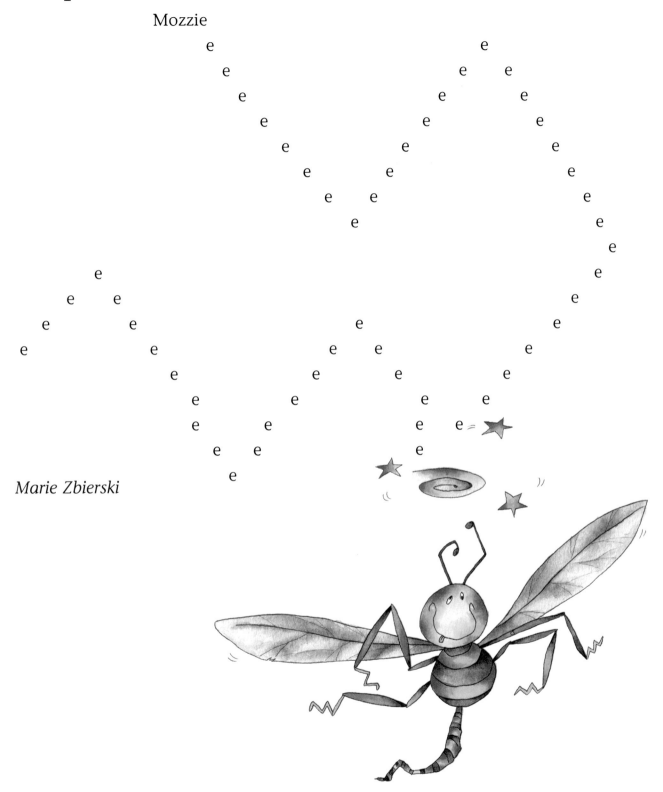

e e
e e e
e e e
e e e
e e e
e e e
e e e
e e e e
e e e e
e e
e e e e
e e e e e
e e e e
e e e e e
e e e e
e e e e
e e e e
e e e
e e

Marie Zbierski

O my!

He rocked the boat,
Did Ezra Shank;
These bubbles mark

    o

    o

    o

    o

    o

    o

    o

    o

    o

    o

    o

    o

Where Ezra sank.

Anonymous

2 Responding to the text

Answer the questions from the , or ◢ section.

1. Look at the poem *Snake*. Why do you think it was written like this?

2. Which of the first three poems do you like best? Why?

3. Would you like to fly off with the crows in *Sky Day Dream*? Why/why not?

4. Why do you think *Mosquito* was written in this way?

1. Which of the first three poems do you like best? Why?

2. Look at the poem *Mosquito*. Why do you think it was written in this way?

3. Think of four more words to add to *Sky Day Dream*.

4. How can a snake's body *whisper*?

1. Which poem do you like best? Why?

2. How can a snake's body *whisper*?

3. Look at the shape of *O my!* Why do you think it's written like this?

4. Do you think the shape of the poem helps you to enjoy reading it?

3 Write your own shape poem

Write your own shape poem. Choose a subject for your poem. You can use one of these ideas or an idea of your own.

giraffe rainbow star snail jelly

Follow this pattern:

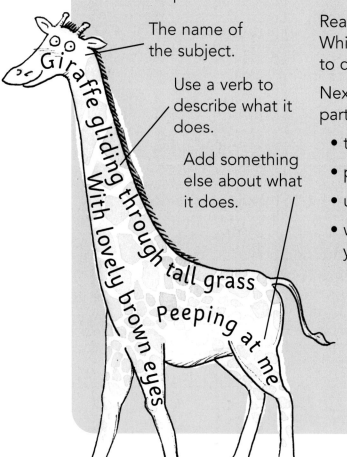

The name of the subject.

Use a verb to describe what it does.

Add something else about what it does.

Giraffe gliding through tall grass
With lovely brown eyes
Peeping at me

Read your poem aloud to yourself. Which words work best? Do you want to change any words?

Next, perform your poem for your partner. Think about:

- talking loudly or quietly.
- pausing and emphasising words.
- using body percussion.
- whether to stand still or move when you perform it.

Remember!
- Think of interesting verbs.
- Reread it to check it makes sense.

What I have learned

- I understand what the term calligram means.
- I can write my own shape poem, using powerful verbs.
- I can rehearse and perform my poem for an audience.

8

Most Magnificent Stories

In this unit, you'll read stories by Roald Dahl and write a review of one of these stories.

Hiding in the Dark

It is well past midnight. Danny is very worried because his father has gone poaching and has not returned home. He decides to take a small car his father is repairing and go to look for him. Then he sees a police car coming towards him.

I didn't dare look round to see if they were stopping and coming back after me. I was certain they would stop. Any policeman in the world would stop if he suddenly passed a small boy in a tiny car chugging along a lonely road at half past two in the morning. My only thought was to get away, to escape, to vanish, though heaven knows how I was going to do that. I pressed my foot harder still on the accelerator. Then all at once I saw in my own dim headlamps the tiny gap in the hedge on my left-hand side. There wasn't time to brake or slow down, so I just yanked the wheel hard over and prayed. The little car swerved violently off the road, leaped

through the gap, hit the rising ground, bounced high in the air, then skidded round sideways behind the hedge and stopped.

The first thing I did was to switch off all my lights. I am not quite sure what made me do this except that I knew that if you are hiding from someone in the dark you don't shine lights all over the place to show where you are. I sat very still in my dark car.

The hedge was a thick one and I couldn't see through it. The car had bounced and skidded sideways in such a way that it was now right off the track. It was behind the hedge and in a sort of field. It was facing back towards the filling-station, tucked in very close to the hedge. I could hear the police car. It had pulled up about fifty yards down the road and now it was backing and turning. The road was far too narrow for it to turn round in one go. Then the roar from the motor got louder and he came back fast with the engine revving and the headlamps blazing.

from **Danny The Champion of the World** *by Roald Dahl*

1 Responding to the text

Answer the questions from the , or section.

1 Why did Danny want to *get away*?

2 How did you feel when you read this story?

3 Why did Danny switch off the car's headlights?

4 Would you like to be Danny? Why/why not?

1 What do you like best about this story? Why?

2 How do you think Danny felt when the police car turned back?

3 Make a list of all the powerful verbs you can find about Danny driving the car, like *yanked* and *swerved*.

4 What do you think will happen when the police car comes back?

1 Do you think this story is spooky or jokey? Give reasons for your answer.

2 Which parts of *Hiding in the Dark* did you find most exciting? Why?

3 What words and phrases do you think are the most exciting? Why?

4 Do you think this story could really happen? Why/why not?

The Wormy Spaghetti

Mr and Mrs Twit are a rather revolting couple. They're always playing tricks on each other.

The next day, to pay Mr Twit back for the frog trick, Mrs Twit sneaked into the garden and dug up some worms. She chose big long ones and put them in a tin and carried the tin back to the house under her apron.

At one o'clock, she cooked spaghetti for lunch and she mixed the worms in with the spaghetti, but only on her husband's plate. The worms didn't show because everything was covered with tomato sauce and sprinkled with cheese.

"Hey, my spaghetti's moving!" cried Mr Twit, poking around in it with his fork.

"It's a new kind," Mrs Twit said, taking a mouthful from her own plate which of course had no worms. "It's called Squiggly Spaghetti. It's delicious. Eat it up while it's nice and hot."

Mr Twit started eating, twisting the long tomato-covered strings around his fork and shovelling them into his mouth. Soon there was tomato sauce all over his hairy chin.

"It's not as good as the ordinary kind," he said, talking with his mouth full. "It's too squishy."

"I find it very tasty," Mrs Twit said. She was watching him from the other end of the table. It gave her great pleasure to watch him eating worms.

"I find it rather bitter," Mr Twit said. "It's got a distinctly bitter flavour. Buy the other kind next time."

Mrs Twit waited until Mr Twit had eaten the whole plateful. Then she said, "You want to know why your spaghetti was squishy?"

Mr Twit wiped the tomato sauce from his beard with a corner of the tablecloth. "Why?" he said.

"And why it had a nasty bitter taste?"

"Why?" he said.

"Because it was *worms*!" cried Mrs Twit, clapping her hands and stamping her feet on the floor and rocking with horrible laughter.

from **The Twits** *by Roald Dahl*

2 Comparing stories by the same author

Read the Roald Dahl stories *Hiding in the Dark* and *The Wormy Spaghetti*.

Talk to your friend about the setting, main character, plot (story) and the main idea (theme) in each story.

Talk about your favourite story and why you like it.

How are the stories similar to each other? How are they different?

Choose one of the Roald Dahl stories. Copy and fill in the table for your story.

Copy and fill in the table for both Roald Dahl stories. Then write a sentence to say how the stories are similar to each other and how they are different.

Title		
Setting Where does the story take place?		
Main characters What kind of people are they? What do you think about them?		
Plot What are the main events?		
Theme What is the main idea of the book?		

3 Looking at compound words

A compound word is a word with a single meaning that is made up of two or more words.

For example, **teapot** is made up of **tea** and **pot**.

❶ Match each word in the red box to a word in the green box to make a compound word.

❷ Make a list of all the words you have found.

❸ Choose one and write it in a sentence.

tea	man
lady	time
finger	lamps
bed	paper
police	brow
head	bell
news	pot
eye	bird
door	nail

❶ Find four compound words in *Hiding in the Dark*.

❷ Make a list of the words you have found.

❸ Think of two more compound words of your own and write them down.

❹ Then use one of them in a sentence.

❶ Work with a partner.

❷ Make a list of all the compound words you can find in *Hiding in the Dark*.

❸ Think of five compound words of your own and write them down.

❹ Then use two of them in a sentence.

4 Planning a book review

You're going to write a review of *The Wormy Spaghetti* for younger children. Make notes about the story for your review.

Use these headings to help you:

Title:

Author:

Main characters:

Tell the story in your own words:

Beginning:

Middle:

End:

I liked/disliked this book because:

Reviewed by:

You're going to write a review of one of the Roald Dahl stories for someone your own age. Make notes about the book for your review. Make sure you make notes for all the information in the checklist.

Checklist

- ✔ Title
- ✔ Author
- ✔ Setting
- ✔ Main ideas
- ✔ Plot – what happens in the story
- ✔ Your feelings
- ✔ Star rating
- ✔ Reviewed by (your name)

5 Writing a book review

Use the notes you made in Activity 4 to write your review. Talk with your partner about what to write in each paragraph. Try to write one or two sentences for each paragraph.

Paragraph 1 – title and something about the author

Paragraph 2 – main characters

Paragraph 3 – your favourite part of the story

Paragraph 4 – your feelings

Use the notes you made in Activity 4 to help you write a review in paragraphs. Write at least one sentence for each paragraph.

Paragraph 1 – introduction

Paragraph 2 – the setting

Paragraph 3 – main characters

Paragraph 4 – the plot

Remember!

- Don't give away all the details of the plot (story). Keep the reader guessing.

- Involve the reader by asking questions like "Can you guess why...?"

- Use some quotations (words from the story) to add interest.

- Give reasons why you liked or disliked the book.

- Write in sentences that start with a capital letter and end with a full stop.

What I have learned

- I can listen to my partner and give my own opinions.

- I can say why some stories are the same and some are different.

- I can make notes and use them to write a book review in paragraphs.

In the Post

9

In this unit, you'll read different types of letters and learn how to write your own letter to a favourite author.

Here are some different types of letters. The style of each letter is different because of its purpose (why it's written) and its audience (the person who it's written to).

16 Kensington Drive,
Morwick Green,
West Yorks

7th April

Dear Sam,

I hope you're enjoying the holiday and everyone is well. Mum says to tell your mum that she'll be glad when we all go back to school, but then she would, wouldn't she?

Yesterday we had a wonderful trip to the National Museum of Photography, Film and Television in Bradford. They have an enormous cinema screen for special films, called Imax. When I say enormous, I mean ENORMOUS! It's three stories high and when you're watching a film you can turn your head to look up, down and sideways. We saw a film called *Grand Canyon*. It was like being there. I mean <u>really</u> being there. We were at the bottom of the canyon and you could look up and see the canyon rim high above you. It was incredible! You really must come over soon and I'll take you (to the museum that is!).

That's all I've got time for now. Dad says I've got to tidy up my room. I suppose that means pushing more stuff under the bed!

See you soon!

Your mate,

Danny

Tolby Toys
Victoria Industrial Estate
Penventon,
Cornwall
88XX 1QQ

1 Southwood Close,
Rothlea,
Suffolk

31st March

Dear Sir/Madam,

I saw your advertisement in the Rothlea Echo and would be grateful if you would send me your catalogue.

I would also like to take advantage of your free gift offer for my early reply.

Yours faithfully,

Charlie Gaw

6, Bramley Gardens

Hi Lee,

I'm having a barbecue on Saturday and I'd love you to come, if you can make it. It'll start at about two o'clock.

Looking forward to seeing you,

Jack

14 Cross St,
Calbury,
Anyshire,
ANY 36XX

10th August

Dear Jo,

Just a quick line to congratulate you on passing your exams. I knew you could do it. Well done!

I'll be up at the weekend to congratulate you personally, when I just might have a little treat for you!

Love,

Aunty Karen

EDITOR – I am writing to reply to F.J.'s letter regarding the danger spot at the junction of Oxford Avenue and Cambridge Crescent. I live at that junction and have witnessed one serious accident and several near misses. In every case it is the speed of the cars that is the problem. Drivers use this route as a shortcut, but it was never intended to carry so many cars. I think speed bumps should be installed immediately.

P. Jones

14 Mayfield Drive,
Nutford,
Wessex
6XP 9PDQ

23rd September

Dear Sir/Madam,

I bought my son a Megaplay game console for his birthday. At first, he enjoyed playing with it, but after a while it developed an annoying fault. Sometimes, halfway through the game, the screen goes blank. After that, he has to switch it off and start again. However, the same thing often happens again.

In view of this, I would like a replacement console or my money back.

Yours faithfully,

Keith Pratt

1 Responding to the text

Answer the questions from the , or section.

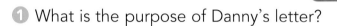

1 What is the purpose of Danny's letter?

2 How does Danny's letter begin and end?

3 Why do you think Keith Pratt's letter starts *Dear Sir/Madam*?

4 Why are the endings in Keith Pratt's and Charlie Gaw's letters different from the endings in Danny's and Aunty Karen's letters?

1 What is the purpose of Charlie Gaw's letter? What is the purpose of Keith Pratt's letter?

2 Why do you think Jack did not write his full address on his letter?

3 What are the differences between Charlie Gaw's letter and Jack's letter?

4 Why do you think there are two addresses in Charlie Gaw's letter?

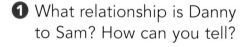

1 What relationship is Danny to Sam? How can you tell?

2 What differences do you notice between P. Jones's letter, Aunty Karen's letter and Keith Pratt's letter?

3 Where do you think you might find a letter to an editor?

4 Write an email and a letter to a friend inviting them to your party. In what ways are they the same? In what ways are they different?

2 Comparing formal and informal letters

In pairs, look again at all the different kinds of letters.

Together, note down who each letter is from and write next to it whether it is formal or informal.

Think about the purpose, greeting, ending and type of language used in each letter. Fill in the information on a chart. Together, decide if the language is formal or informal and say how you can tell.

From	Purpose	Greeting	Ending	Language
Danny				
P. Jones				
Aunty Karen				informal – uses friendly, everyday expressions

3 Looking at connectives

The Farm,
Bitton,
GL1 2DK
1st July

Copy this letter and fill in the missing connectives from the box.

| when | but | and |

Dear Annie,

Thank you for your letter _____ the drawing. I would love to come to your Book Week _____ I am visiting another school that day.

Perhaps we can arrange another date _____ I am not so busy.

Yours sincerely,
D.K. Smith

Copy this letter and fill in the missing connectives.

Use the words in the box. Check that sentences start with a capital letter.

| however   sometimes   but |
| after that   at first |

20 Sloth Avenue,
Wearydale
SLP1 9ZZ

10th July

Dear Sir or Madam,

I bought my husband Ted a Talk-To-Me exercise bike for his birthday. _____ it worked brilliantly ____ then it began to make strange groaning noises when Ted started cycling. _____ the bike would ask to stop and have a rest! _____ the bike said it was tired and needed a little lie down. Ted tried to reset the exercise programme; _____ it is still groaning and grumbling.

In view of this, I would like a replacement bike or my money back.

Yours faithfully,
Lesley Speedwell

4 Writing a letter to an author

Write a letter to your favourite author inviting them to visit your school during a Book Week.

[Write the address on the right-hand side of the letter.]

[Miss a line before writing the date underneath the address.]

Dear [Use the author's title – Mr, Miss, Mrs or Ms.]

[The first paragraph shows the purpose of the letter.]

[The second paragraph might tell the author something about you.]

[The third paragraph might ask the author some questions.]

[The last paragraph repeats the purpose of the letter.]

[Close with a short, polite sentence.]

[End with *Yours sincerely,* followed by your full name.]

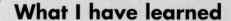

What I have learned

- I can write simple and more complex sentences.

- I can put sentences in an order that makes sense.

- I can identify the audience and write a formal or informal letter.

A Roller Coaster Read

In this unit, you'll read, compare and contrast an adventure story and a mystery story. At the end of the unit, you'll write a short sequel to the adventure story *Skull Island*.

Looking for Zack

Robyn and Ben arrive at Skull Island but there is no sign of Zack, just a mysterious set of footprints and a trail of blood.

The island was still, and silent, save for the gentle splashing of the waves. A bird's plaintive cry broke the silence, making Robyn jump. For some reason she shivered, though the air felt much hotter here than on Paradise.

The island seemed to have a brooding presence. It had seen some terrible things. Robyn remembered the hundreds of slaves who had met their deaths here and shivered again. Even with Ben beside her, she felt inexplicably lonely. There was no sign of Zack's launch. They climbed out of the boat and began to walk up the beach.

"Where should we go first?" Robyn was asking, when Ben gasped. She looked up to see his face turn white.

"Zack?" he croaked. He sounded petrified. Robyn followed to where his finger was pointing. There on the beach in front of them was a set of footprints. Footprints which went up to a sandy path and stopped beside a rock, on which there lay a torn shirt soaked in blood.

——— • ———

"Maybe he just cut himself on something…" Robyn's voice died away. It sounded lame, even to her. "Well, we have to find him," she added, sounding more positive than she felt. "And the sooner the better."

A trail of blood spots led away from the rock along the sandy path. Hearts thumping, they followed it, winding their way steeply up the side of a hill, passing a mass of trees on their right. Once or twice they paused to catch their breath, looking down on the cove.

from Skull Island *by Lesley Sims*

1 Responding to the text

Answer the questions from the , or section.

❶ Which sound made Robyn jump?

❷ What terrible things had Robyn remembered?

❸ Why did Ben and Robyn walk up the beach?

❹ What do you think had happened to Zack?

❶ Read the first sentence aloud to yourself twice. Why did the author decide to write a long sentence like this one?

❷ How can an island see *terrible things*?

❸ How could Robyn feel *inexplicably lonely* if Ben was right beside her?

❹ What do you think had happened to Zack?

❶ Explain why Robyn shivered twice.

❷ How could she feel *inexplicably lonely* if Ben was right beside her?

❸ Look up the word *petrified* in a dictionary and say why the author chose this word.

❹ What do you think had happened to Zack?

Jacqueline Hyde

Jacqueline Hyde is a well-behaved girl: polite, punctual, clean, tidy and helpful. Then one day she finds an old medicine bottle in Grandma's attic.

There was some stuff in it. Thickish liquid that moved like treacle. There wasn't much – about two centimetres. The cork had been pushed so far in I couldn't get a grip so I took it under the skylight and worked at it with my nails, and after a bit I got it out.

It came away with a pop. I sniffed it but it just smelt old so I sniffed the bottleneck. It smelt sort of sharp. Fruity. Bit like lime juice. It made my nostrils tingle, and the tingle seemed to pass behind my eyes into my forehead and then spread across the inside of my skull till it reached the nape of my neck and trickled down my spine.

It's hard to describe how it made me feel, and you wouldn't believe me anyway. I felt … excited. I was bursting with energy, like Popeye after a spinach fix. Ready for anything.

There was this mirror. A flyspecked full-length mirror that swivelled in a frame. I looked at myself. I thought I'd look different but I didn't so I stuck my tongue out. "Just look at you," I sneered. "You're so *good*, aren't you, Jacqueline Hyde? So yuckily, sick-makingly good. See how *clean* you've kept yourself, even in this mucky old attic. Grandma *will* be pleased."

I hated my reflection. *Hated* it. I know it sounds daft but I did. There was a flatiron on the floor. A rusty flatiron. I bent down and grabbed it and snarled, "Here, Jacqueline Good – catch." I got that mirror dead-centre and it shattered, spraying glittering

fragments everywhere. The iron rebounded and crashed on the dusty floorboards and I heard Grandma call out, "Jacqueline – what's happening up there? Are you all right?"

Oh, I was all right, all right. *More* than all right. For the first time in my life I was alive. Fully alive. I headed for the door.

from Jacqueline Hyde *by Robert Swindells*

2 Responding to the text

Answer the questions from the , or section.

1. Where is the mystery set?

2. Look at the picture and write a sentence describing the attic.

3. Why do you think Jacqueline hated her reflection?

4. Do you prefer the good or the bad Jacqueline? Why?

1. Where does the mystery start?

2. What happened when Jacqueline smelt the bottle?

3. How do you think it made her feel?

4. Where did Jacqueline feel a *tingle*?

1. Write a sentence to describe what the *stuff* that was in the bottle looked like.

2. Make a list of the words describing the smell of the liquid.

3. What does *Popeye after a spinach fix* mean?

4. How do you think Jacqueline felt after she had sniffed the mixture?

3 Changing from first to third person

Pronouns are words that can be used in place of a person's proper name. There are first, second and third person pronouns.

First person

we ourselves us me myself us I

Second person

you yourself

Third person

it themselves them herself him he she they

Copy out these sentences. Choose a pronoun from the list below and put it in the correct place in the sentence. Then say if your sentence is written in the first or third person. The first one has been done for you.

she   my   her   myself

❶ It made ..her. nostrils tingle. (third person)

❷ I looked at ......

❸ A sour taste poured into ...... mouth.

❹ ...... was all right.

Copy these sentences from *Jacqueline Hyde* and underline the pronouns.

> I looked at myself. I thought I'd look different but I didn't so I stuck my tongue out. "Just look at you," I sneered.

Next rewrite the sentences in the third person.

Change the second paragraph of *Jacqueline Hyde* into the third person, starting at *It came away with a pop* and ending at *and trickled down my spine.*

Remember!

- Check you've changed all the pronouns.
- Check you've changed the verb endings.

4 Think/pair/share

Imagine that you are Jacqueline's grandma. How would you explain to Jacqueline's teacher what happened to Jacqueline in the attic? Working in pairs, take turns to be Grandma and the teacher. When it's your turn to be the teacher, make sure you have lots of questions to ask Grandma.

5 Writing a letter from Grandma

Now you're going to write a letter from Grandma to Jacqueline's teacher, Mr Whittaker, explaining what happened to Jacqueline in the attic and how she has changed. The first part of the letter has been done for you.

Talk to your friend about what would be in the letter. Then write some sentences to finish the letter.

Think about what would be in the letter and write some sentences to finish it.

Remember!

- Check that you are using the right pronouns.
- Check your punctuation.
- Read your letter back to yourself. Does it make sense?

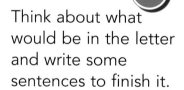

15th May

Dear Mr Whittaker,

I am writing to tell you about something strange that happened to Jacqueline last week. She told me she had been up in my attic and found an old bottle. When she pulled out the cork, she sniffed it. Then ...

6 Writing a sequel to *Skull Island*

You're going to write a sequel to *Skull Island*.

Your adventure story should have at least three paragraphs. Use these characters: Robyn, Mrs Curtis (Robyn's mother) and Ben. You can use the setting of Skull Island or choose your own. Before you start to write, decide:

• how your story starts.

• what the problem will be and how it will be solved.

• how your story ends.

Use connective words to link your paragraphs.

Here are some to choose from:

seconds later	suddenly	next	meanwhile
immediately	finally	at that moment	after that

Remember!

● Use interesting words to describe the setting and the characters.

● Write in sentences that make sense.

● Use dialogue to move the story along.

● Choose powerful verbs to make it exciting.

● Link your story together with connective words.

● Make sure your story has a problem and a resolution.

What I have learned

• I can listen and respond to ideas.

• I can use role play to develop my ideas.

• I understand the main features of adventure stories and mystery stories.

• I can write a sequel to an adventure story.

Gathering Information

In this unit, you'll learn about the features of non-fiction texts, and how to make notes and use them to write about a festival you know really well. You'll also learn about using a dictionary, a thesaurus and other alphabetical texts.

Diwali

Diwali (or sometimes Divali) is the Hindu festival of light.

Diwali is a Hindu festival and the themes of Diwali tell us about what Hindus believe. Hinduism centres on the worship of God, who can be worshipped in different ways through different Hindu gods. The most important thing for a Hindu is to love and please God – by living a good life, by setting up shrines at home, by frequent prayers and by celebrating the many Hindu festivals. Diwali is such a festival.

Diwali is the Hindu festival of light. The word Diwali is short for dipawali, which means "row of lights". Diwali is celebrated during late October or early November, when it gets dark early and the nights are cold, long and dark. Hindus enjoy preparing for festivals as much as they enjoy celebrating them. They can start preparing for Diwali a month before the festivities begin and the celebrations can last for up to five days.

At Diwali, the dark nights are lit up. Houses have welcoming lamps at all their doors and windows, and multicoloured lights decorate the streets. The temples are covered with tiny rows of lights and the sky is ablaze with fireworks. Shop windows are piled with different-coloured sweets and everybody wears their brightest clothes.

During Diwali people put welcoming lights at their doors and windows.

Diwali is celebrated for different reasons all over India because different gods are honoured in different areas. However, all the different Diwali festivities have a lot in common. They celebrate the triumph of good over evil, light over darkness, life over death. It is a time of hope and new beginnings.

from **Diwali** *by Kerena Marchant*

Diwali is the Hindu festival of light.

1 Responding to the text

Answer the questions from the , or section.

1. Is this an information text or a story? How do you know?
2. What does the word *Diwali* mean?
3. Is Diwali a festival like Christmas or Eid?
4. Draw a picture of things you would see at night during Diwali.
5. How long does Diwali last?

1. Is this an information text or a story? How do you know?
2. What does the word *Diwali* mean?
3. Write down the names of some other festivals you know.
4. Write down three facts that tell the reader what happens during Diwali.
5. What is the purpose of Diwali?

1. Is this an information text or a story? How do you know?
2. What does the word *Diwali* mean?
3. How would you know that Diwali was taking place if you visited India in November?
4. In what ways does Diwali remind you of any other festivals?
5. What is the purpose of Diwali?

2 Using a chart to collect information

KWL charts are very useful to help with reading and writing an information text.

> **K** is what you know.
>
> **W** is what you want to find out.
>
> **L** is what you have learned from the text.

Work in a group to fill in the chart for *The Camel Fair*.

Think about what you know about camels and write this in the first column.

Next, think about what you want to find out about camels and write this in the second column.

Read the text *The Camel Fair* on pages 84–85 and then decide what you have learned about camels. Write this in the third column.

KWL chart

What we know	What we want to know	What we have learned

3 Role play

Choose a festival you know really well. Copy the table and prepare some questions and answers about the festival.

Questions	Answers
What is the name of the festival?	
When does it take place?	
Why does it take place?	
How long does it last?	
What special things happen?	
What do you enjoy most about the festival?	

In pairs, take turns to interview each other about the festival. When it's your turn to do the interview, note down the key words from your partner's answers.

Questions	Key words
What is the name of the festival?	

You can change the questions or add some more of your own.

The Camel Fair

This information text describes a famous camel fair and provides some interesting facts about camels.

Journey to Pushkar

The Pushkar Camel Fair is very famous. People come long distances to buy and sell camels, but they also come to enjoy themselves.

In Rajasthan camels are very important, especially for people who live in the desert and in villages. People use camels to get themselves and their things from place to place, they drink camel milk and camel hair is used to make rugs, tents and clothing. Even camel dung is collected, dried and sold as fuel for cooking fires.

At the Camel Fair

Each day at the Camel Fair there are camel auctions, where traders buy and sell camels. There are camel shows and camel races, too.

All the camels are decorated and look quite amazing. They wear necklaces of tinsel and flowers, and some of them are painted with beautiful patterns in henna. There are rows and rows of stalls nearby selling bells, ribbons and other decorations just for the camels!

Camel facts

- Camels are very strong mammals with wide, padded feet. They have bushy eyebrows and long eyelashes to protect their eyes from desert sand.
- A camel with one hump is called a dromedary, or Arabian camel.
- A camel with two humps is called a Bactrian camel.
- The wild Bactrian camel is an endangered species.
- A camel's hump contains fat, not water, and the camel can go without food and water for three or four days.

long eyelashes and
bushy eyebrows

large nostrils that can
open and close

a fat-filled hump

thick, shaggy fur

**An Arabian
camel**

**A Bactrian
camel**

two-toed feet with
leathery pads

a long tail

from **The Camel Fair** *by Wendy Cooling*

4 Using diagrams to give information

You're going make a Camel Information Sheet for a
six-year-old to read.

- Choose one of the camels and write its name at the top of
  your sheet.

- Draw its outline in the middle of your sheet.

- Choose five interesting facts.

- Write five **easy to understand** sentences inside the camel's shape
  – use your own words!

- Write five labels for the camel – decide what is important to
  label.

- Check that a six-year-old can understand the information.

5 Using a dictionary

① A dictionary is divided into four parts. Each part is called a quartile. You'll need four blank bookmarks for this activity.

Open your dictionary at letter A. Take one of the bookmarks and write the letter A on it. Then write the words *first quartile* on your bookmark. Put your bookmark at the beginning, at letter A.

Open your dictionary in the middle. Which letter is at the start of the page? Write this letter on another bookmark and then write the words *third quartile* on it. Put your bookmark here.

Open the dictionary a quarter of the way through. Which letter is at the start of the page? Write this letter on a bookmark and write the words *second quartile* on it. Put your bookmark here.

Open the dictionary three-quarters of the way through. Which letter is at the start of the page? Write this letter on a bookmark and write the words *fourth quartile* on it. Place your bookmark here.

② In which quartile would you see these words?

| sit | pet | wise | dog | cap | net |

③ Copy this chart, then write each word in the correct quartile.

First quartile	Second quartile	Third quartile	Fourth quartile

④ Now add these words to your chart.

| tree | ball | holly | mess | rust | drag |

Now add these words. | quiet | ice | gate | eel |

Now add these words. | yacht | kettle | open | job |

6 Exploring the meaning of words

Look at the following words with your partner:

| nail   jungle   junction   circle   famous   satellite   picnic |

Create a chart like the one below. Discuss what you think each word means.

Look up the word in your dictionary. Fill in the word, your definition and the dictionary definition. If the word has more than one meaning, add all the meanings.

Use three of the words.

Use four of the words.

Use all the words.

Word	Your definition	Dictionary definition
nail	something that you hammer into wood	
nail	something at the end of fingers and toes	

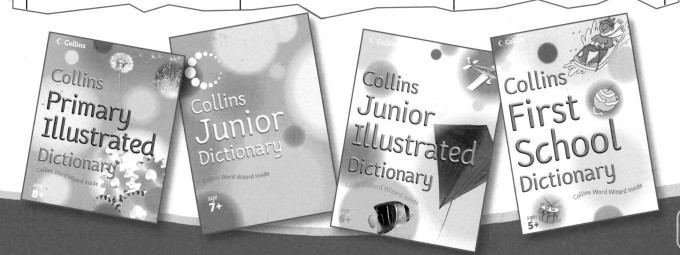

7 Writing about your favourite festival

There are lots of different festivals. Write an information text about your favourite festival. Choose one that you know well.

Use the underlined key words in the questions below to help you write four paragraphs describing your favourite festival. You can use your own questions if you want to.

Questions:

Paragraph 1 (Introduction)

<u>Why</u> does the <u>festival</u> take place?

Paragraph 2

<u>When</u> and <u>how often does it happen?</u>

<u>Why</u> does it happen at a <u>particular time of year</u>?

Paragraph 3

<u>What</u> can you <u>see, hear, smell and taste</u> during the festival?

Paragraph 4 (Ending)

<u>What</u> do <u>you</u> like best about the festival?

Your paragraphs might look like this:

Paragraph 1 (Introduction)	the reason for the festival
Paragraph 2	when the festival takes place
Paragraph 3	special things about the festival
Paragraph 4 (Ending)	my favourite part

In pairs, write or rehearse aloud one sentence for each paragraph.

Write two sentences for each paragraph heading.

Write two or three sentences for each paragraph heading.

Remember!

- Work in pairs. Say your sentence aloud to your partner.

- Write the sentence on your mini-whiteboard and check it carefully.

- Ask your partner to check your sentence.

- Make any corrections and write the sentence in your information text.

What I have learned

- I can talk about what I have learned.

- I can make useful notes on a non-fiction text.

- I understand that a dictionary is divided into four quartiles.

- I can write a non-fiction text clearly in paragraphs.

12 Puzzle It Out!

In this unit, you'll read word puzzles, riddle poems and poems that play with words, and write your own poem.

Word puzzles

Can you work out these riddles? Read them with a friend – two heads are better than one!

A house full, a hole full,
You cannot catch a bowlful.

Round as a biscuit;
Busy as a bee;
Prettiest little thing
You ever did see.

Runs all day and never walks,
Often murmurs, never talks.
It has a bed, but never sleeps,
It has a mouth, but never eats.

What has a tongue but can't talk?

Which two animals go with you everywhere?

Little Nancy Etticoat
In a white petticoat
And a red rose.
The longer she stands,
The shorter she grows.

Riddle me! Riddle me! What is that:
Over your head and under your hat?

UR 2 GOOD

UR 2 GOOD
2 ME
2 BE
4 GOT
10

Michael Rosen

90

Two Terrible Tongue Twisters

Learn these and say them fast!

Thomas a Tattamus took two T's
To tie two tups to two tall trees,
To frighten the terrible Thomas a Tattamus!
Tell me how many T's there are in all that.

Billy Bunter bought a buttered biscuit.
If Billy Bunter bought a buttered biscuit,
Where's the buttered biscuit
That Billy Bunter bought?

1 Responding to the text

Answer the questions from the , or section.

❶ Copy out one of the riddles in your best writing. Write its answer.

❷ Write out the words for *UR 2 GOOD* in full.

❸ Which is your favourite riddle? Why?

❹ Say the tongue twister *Thomas a Tattamus* aloud to a friend as fast as you can. Do you know any more tongue twisters?

❶ What are the two animals that go with you everywhere? [Clue: look at the picture!]

❷ What two kinds of *tongue* is the boy in the picture talking about?

❸ Which do you like best, the riddles or the tongue twisters? Why?

❹ Write out the words for *UR 2 GOOD* in full.

❶ How could you write the word *ate* as a number? Can you think of any other words like this?

❷ Work out the answer to the *Thomas a Tattamus* riddle.

❸ Write a tongue twister of your own.

❹ Which do you like best, the riddles or the tongue twisters? Why?

2 Homonyms

Homonyms are words that sound the same but have different meanings, like in some of the riddles.

For example:

calf

calf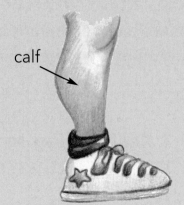

Sometimes the words sound the same but are spelt differently.
For example:

eight ⟶ ate

two ⟶ too

Find these words in your dictionary and write two meanings for each word.

rock   wave   train

Choose one of the words and write two sentences to show each meaning.

Find these words in your dictionary and write two meanings for each word.

book   watch

Say a sentence to your partner for each meaning of these words.

For example:

I can tell the time with my watch.

Write the homonyms for these words.

write   to   there

Write a sentence for each word to show its meaning.

3 Riddling homonyms

Work in pairs. Use the two meanings of these words to complete the riddles.

❶ set

a) to become solid

b) to go below the horizon at sunset

> Why is the sun like jelly?
>
> Because …

❷ lighter

a) not as heavy

b) not as dark

> Why was the box easier to carry at sunrise?
>
> Because …

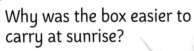

❸ fast

a) moving very quickly

b) showing a later time than the real time

> Why is the clock like a
> _____?
>
> Because …

4 Onomatopoeia

Onomatopoeia is when words are used that sound like the thing they describe, like *clang*, *hiccup* and *sizzle*.

Choose one of these objects and draw its shape. Write onomatopoeia words (sound words) for the object inside the shape.

| a bee   a snake   a dog   a bell |

For example:

Bang   Crash
Thump

Two poems by the same author

*Both these poems are by Judith Nicholls – a riddle poem and
a patterned poem.*

Riddle

I am
pear-drop
space-hopper,
rest-on-a-tail;
fast as a rocket,
and what's in my pocket
small as a snail?
I'm shorter than elephant,
taller than man;
I hop-step-and-jump
as no creature can.
My jacket is fur,
my pocket too;
a joey hides there...
I am
KANGAROO!

Judith Nicholls

Teacher said ...

You can use
    mumbled and muttered
    groaned, grumbled and uttered
    professed, droned or stuttered
       ... but don't use SAID!

You can use
    rant or recite
    yell, yodel or snort
    bellow, murmur or moan
    you can use grunt or just groan
       ... but don't use SAID!

You can use
    hum, howl and hail
    scream, screech, shriek or bawl
    squeak, snivel or squeal
      with a blood-curdling wail
         ... but don't use SAID!
         ... SAID my teacher.

Judith Nicholls

5 Writing a poem with synonyms

Synonyms are words that sound different but have a similar meaning. For example, *giggle* and *chuckle* are synonyms of *laugh*.

Read the poem *Teacher said …* . Think of some more synonyms that you can use instead of *said* and write another verse.

Use *Teacher said …* as a pattern for your own poem using synonyms. Use this idea for the first verse or choose one of your own.

Teacher said …

You can use

    left, departed, set off

    travelled and journeyed

    vanished, disappeared or escaped

       … but don't use WENT!

For verses 2, 3, and 4, think of synonyms for *walked*, *ran* and *moved*.

Remember!

- *Use Teacher said … as a model for your poem.*
- Think about how your poem starts and ends.
- Read your poem aloud to see if it sounds good.
- Share it with your partner.

6 Writing a riddle poem

Write a riddle poem about an animal you know well.

❶ First, think about the animal that you're going to write about (the answer to your riddle). List as many words as you can think of about your animal.

❷ Pick three important words from your list and find synonyms for them in your thesaurus.

❸ Imagine you are your animal. What can you see, hear, feel and smell? What do you do all day? What do you like doing best? Note down your ideas.

❹ Look again at *Riddle*. Use it as a model and start to write your riddle poem.

❺ When you're writing, try to use interesting words. You could use:
  - **alliteration** (words that start with the same letter or sound).
  - **onomatopoeia** (words whose sound is like their meaning).
  - **similes** (words that compare your animal to something, like fast as a rocket).

❻ Try out your riddle poem on a friend. Can they guess what animal it is?

Remember!

- *Use Judith Nicholls's Riddle poem as a model.*
- *Think about how her poem starts and ends.*
- *Give clues but don't give away too much information too soon!*

What I have learned

- I can read and recite poems that play with language.
- I can write poems that use synonyms, alliteration and onomatopoeia.
- I can perform my own poems for an audience.